PREGNANCY

Kirsten Lamb

HODDER
Wayland

an imprint of Hodder Children's Books

© 2001 White-Thomson Publishing Ltd

White-Thomson Publishing Ltd,
2-3 St Andrew's Place, Lewes,
East Sussex BN7 1UP

Published in Great Britain in 2001 by Hodder Wayland, an imprint of Hodder Children's Books.

This book was produced for White-Thomson Publishing Ltd by Ruth Nason.

Design: Carole Binding
Picture research: Glass Onion Pictures

The right of Kirsten Lamb to be identified as the author of this work has been asserted by her in accordance with the Copyright, Designs and Patents Act 1988.

British Library Cataloguing in Publication Data
Lamb, Kirsten
  Pregnancy. - (Health Issues)
  1. Pregnancy - Juvenile literature
  I. Title
  618.2

ISBN 0 7502 3181 5

Printed in Italy by G. Canale & C.S.p.A.

Hodder Children's Books
A division of Hodder Headline Limited
338 Euston Road, London NW1 3BH

Acknowledgements
The author and publishers thank the following for their permission to reproduce photographs and illustrations: Corbis Images: pages 23 (Laura Dwight), 37 (April Saul), 38 (right), 42 (Arvind Garg), 43 (Bettmann), 49 (Pablo Corral V), 58 (left) (Owen Franken), 58 (right) (Liba Taylor); Angela Hampton Family Life Pictures: cover and pages 1, 5, 16, 19, 20, 22, 24, 32, 33, 35, 41, 46; Impact Photo (Robin Laurance): page 38 (left); Panos Pictures: page 57 (Giacomo Pirozzi); Photofusion: pages 4 (Paul Baldesare), 11 (Paul Baldesare), 34 (Tim Dub), 40 (Paul Baldesare), 59 (Liam Bailey); Popperfoto: pages 15, 26 (bottom), 53, 56; Science Photo Library: pages 6 (D. Phillips), 13 (Hattie Young), 14 (Dr G. Moscoso), 26 (top) (Jim Varney), 27 (James Stevenson), 54 (Richard Rawlins/Custom Medical Stock Photo); Wayland Picture Library: pages 7 (Michael Courtney), 9 (Zak Waters), 10 (Michael Courtney), 12 (Zul Mukhida), 21 (Michael Courtney), 45, 47 (Jeff Issac Greenberg); www.JohnBirdsall.co.uk: pages 28, 29. The illustration on page 8 was drawn by Michael Courtney. The illustrations on pages 17, 30, 50, 51 and 52 were drawn by Carole Binding.

Contents

Introduction
Why should I know about pregnancy?

Pregnancy is an exciting, normal and natural event. It is the wonderful creation of a new life and culminates in the birth of a new baby.

Is knowing about pregnancy relevant to young people at school? The answer must be yes. Many young people will want to think about their future and the idea of a family of their own, to work out how to plan that, to avoid pregnancy at the wrong time and to think about the consequences of pregnancy. Young people of school age do get pregnant. Has that been their informed choice or did events overtake them? Knowing the facts and understanding the issues that surround pregnancy, as they may affect you, helps you to make your own choices about your future.

Read on and see how a normal pregnancy starts, progresses and ends in delivery of a baby. There are ways that pregnancy can be planned for, to help to achieve this aim. Even as a teenager, the way that you live may influence your future ability to have children.

Having a baby has a huge impact on a person's life. Babies and their parents all have needs that have to be fulfilled. Ask yourself what it would be like to be pregnant and become a parent when still a teenager of school age. Would you be able to fulfil the needs of your baby and yourself?

Chapter 5 looks at the options for people who get pregnant when they don't want to be. Teenagers in this situation find it difficult to know how to seek help. Termination of pregnancy can be a way out, but there are many different feelings about the ethics of termination of pregnancy.

Unwanted pregnancy can usually be avoided. Teenagers are just starting out on developing close relationships, and feelings can be hard to understand because they are all new. These feelings can be very powerful. Talking to your parents about them may be difficult. At school you will have lessons about sexual relationships, but you may feel embarrassed talking about these matters in front of your class mates.

Thinking about your own sexuality, and understanding the impact that it has on you, can help to avoid problems like unwanted pregnancy. Understanding can make you more able to talk about these subjects with your parents or with your partner. It can help you to be able to choose when you start to have sexual relationships, and to know how you can get sexual pleasure without risking unwanted pregnancy.

Contraception is safe and available. Knowing about it will enable you to work out how to get hold of the right contraceptive for you. You have the right to choose what is right for you and when the time is right for you.

What about the future? The final chapter looks at developments in contraception and fertility management that might happen in your lifetime, and challenges you to think about some questions of what is 'right' for human life.

The facts

I'd rather know what is real fact than some of the rubbish you hear.

1 Conception
How pregnancy begins

Two halves make a whole, or the genetics of conception

Technically speaking, the very first thing that must happen to make a baby is the meeting of sperm and egg. Sperm are the seeds that come from males after puberty. Eggs are the seeds that females produce. Each seed (the sperm or the egg) contains half the genetic material needed to make one human cell.

That human cell contains a nucleus, which in turn contains chromosomes – microscopic threads made up of about 2,000 genes each. Chromosomes contain all the individual genetic information that makes us precisely who we are. They determine, for example, our hair and eye colour, and our blood group.

Sperm and egg

A single sperm penetrates the wall of an egg. This false-coloured picture is magnified by about 800.

Girl or boy?

All human cells contain 46 chromosomes, consisting of 44 ordinary chromosomes and 2 sex chromosomes known as X or Y chromosomes. The first cell of a new baby is created by joining a sperm and an egg, each of which provides 22 ordinary chromosomes and one sex chromosome. The sex chromosome in a sperm may be either an X or a Y. The sex chromosome in an egg is always an X. If a sperm containing an X chromosome fertilizes an egg, the baby will be a girl. If a sperm containing a Y chromosome fertilizes an egg, the baby will be a boy.

Sperm production

Sperm are produced in the testes of men. The two testes sit in the sac called the scrotum, which is a bag of skin. The temperature inside the scrotum is less than that in the body, and this cooler temperature is necessary for sperm to be produced. The making of sperm, or the male seed, is very different from egg production in females. Sperm are made continuously in the testes after puberty. Millions of sperm are produced. Each sperm looks a little like a tadpole, the head containing the genetic material and the moving tail allowing the sperm to swim. The sperm are minute. Each sperm is 1/25 of a millimetre long!

Sperm have to be able to swim in order to find their target, the egg. Only healthy active sperm will achieve this. Millions of sperm are released during ejaculation. Ejaculation is the release of sperm-containing fluid (semen) from the penis, which occurs during sexual intercourse or masturbation.

Semen analysis

A man's production of sperm can be checked by examining a sample of semen. The ejaculated semen is looked at under a microscope. The sperm are counted and examined to check that they appear normal and that they are active and swim well. This is called semen analysis.

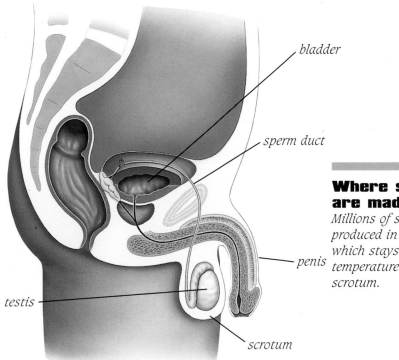

bladder

sperm duct

penis

testis

scrotum

Where sperm are made

Millions of sperm are produced in the testis, which stays at the right temperature inside the scrotum.

During sexual intercourse semen is ejaculated from the end of the penis into the vagina of the female. The sperm then start their journey to meet the egg.

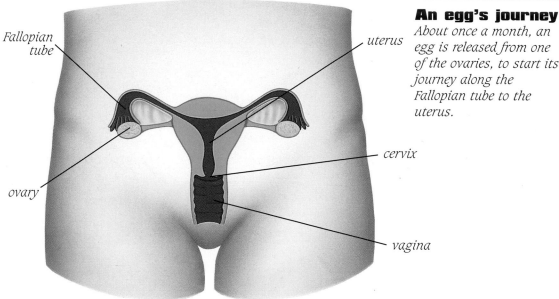

Fallopian tube

ovary

uterus

cervix

vagina

An egg's journey

About once a month, an egg is released from one of the ovaries, to start its journey along the Fallopian tube to the uterus.

Egg production

This is very different from male sperm production. Girls are born with a finite or set number of eggs in each ovary. The eggs have been produced while the baby girl was developing in her mother's womb. By puberty, the number of eggs available to mature is about 40,000 – a small number compared with the millions of sperm produced by the male.

Ovaries are the female equivalent of the testes, but lie inside the pelvis, at the base of the abdomen. Girls have two ovaries, one on each side. The eggs sit in the ovaries, dormant or asleep, until puberty and the start of periods. The pattern of a girl's periods is called the menstrual cycle. This pattern repeats itself every month. First, one egg starts to ripen in either one or the other ovary. Halfway through the time from one period to the next, this egg is released from the ovary. This release is called ovulation. The egg is then swept up by the fluffy (technically known as fimbriated) end of the Fallopian tube.

Other things take place in a girl's body at ovulation. The lining of the womb (technically known as the uterus) starts to get thicker. This is in preparation for pregnancy. If the egg is fertilized, it will attach itself to the inside wall of the uterus, where it will grow during pregnancy. The thickened lining of the uterus makes it more possible for the fertilized egg to attach. Also, at ovulation, the mucus or jelly-like substance in the cervix gets thinner. This makes it easier for the sperm to swim through the cervix to meet the egg.

If the egg is not fertilized and pregnancy does not take place, then about two weeks after ovulation the whole process switches off. The thickened lining of the uterus is shed as the blood in a period, and then the whole cycle starts again.

Period pain

It is normal for periods to cause some pain. If taking a painkiller and/or holding a hot-water bottle against the pain does not bring relief, your doctor can offer other solutions.

Hormones

For the female reproductive system to work properly, it is vital that hormones are produced in the ovaries. Hormones are chemicals that travel from the place where they are produced (in this case the ovary) to take a message to another part of the body (in this case the uterus). The ovary always produces oestrogen, the main female hormone. At ovulation, or the release of the egg from the ovary, a gap is left in the ovary. This becomes known as the corpus luteum (Latin for 'yellow body') as it looks yellow within the ovary. The corpus luteum is a hormone-making factory. It now starts making progesterone, the other female hormone. Progesterone is responsible for thickening the lining of the uterus to let the fertilized egg attach.

Fertilization, or egg meets sperm

During sexual intercourse, sperm are ejaculated into the top part of the female vagina. Luckily, the sperm have a very mobile tail and so they are able to swim through the cervix and up through the uterus to try to meet the egg. Meanwhile the egg has no way of propelling itself. It has been swept up by the fimbriated end of the Fallopian tube and is drifting down towards the uterus. For fertilization to take place, the sperm must meet the egg in the Fallopian tube. The head of the swimming sperm attaches itself to the egg. This is the process of fertilization. The two parts of genetic material join and then the resulting cell is able to start dividing to start the process of making a baby.

Dividing cells

After fertilization, the single cell starts to divide, making two, then four, then eight, then sixteen cells, and so on. See page 14 for how the cells become a baby.

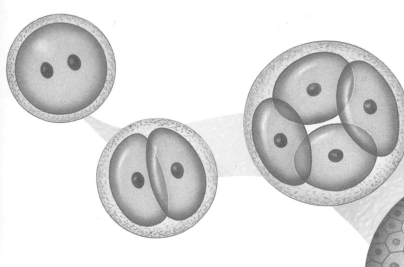

How does a woman know that she is pregnant?

When the woman's egg has been fertilized by the man's sperm, things start to change in the woman's body. More and more progesterone is released, and the thickened lining of the uterus allows the fertilized egg – now called the embryo – to attach itself. Once attached, the embryo can start to grow and develop into a baby by getting nutrients and oxygen directly from the blood of its mother.

The uterus and growing embryo need a continuous supply of progesterone at the start of pregnancy, to let the pregnancy progress. To ensure that this happens, the uterus, at the site of implantation, produces another hormone – HCG or Human Chorionic Gonadotrophin. This tells the ovary to keep producing enough progesterone to maintain the pregnancy.

The effect of all this hormonal activity is to switch off further ovulation and therefore to switch off the menstrual cycle and periods. So, the first thing that most women notice after they have conceived is that they miss a period. Very occasionally, some women will have a small amount of light bleeding at the time they expect a period. But, for most women, menstrual bleeding stops with conception.

Influences

Powerful feelings, a party atmosphere and alcohol all influence our actions.

Gemma and Jim

Jim and Gemma, who are both 16, have been going out for a couple of months. At the last party they went to, things got a bit carried away and one thing led to another. Sex was OK, but they had both had a bit to drink and so it was all over rather quickly and Gemma didn't remember much the next day. Now she is in a panic. Her period is late and for the last couple of years they have been regular. She doesn't feel right. She keeps feeling sick, her breasts are sore, and her bra feels too tight. What does she do next? Can she talk to Jim about it? Perhaps if she doesn't think about it, it will go away. But she could be pregnant.

Gemma's late period certainly means that she could be pregnant. If she is, then the high levels of progesterone will be causing other changes in her body. She may notice:

- nausea or 'morning sickness'. Morning sickness is not an accurate description, as women can feel or be sick at any time of day when they are pregnant.
- breast changes. The breasts get larger and become painful. This is the start of the process of producing milk for breast-feeding.
- urinary frequency. Most women need to pass urine more frequently during pregnancy.
- constipation. Progesterone makes the muscle in the gut more sluggish and therefore makes it more difficult to open bowels.
- feeling tired. This is very common in early pregnancy.
- having fads about foods. Some women crave certain foods and dislike the thought of others while they are pregnant.
- vaginal discharge. This is an increased loss of clear fluid from the vagina, causing staining on underwear or maybe needing a pad. The discharge occurs because the vaginal lining has also been stimulated by the pregnancy hormones to thicken, and to produce more fluid.

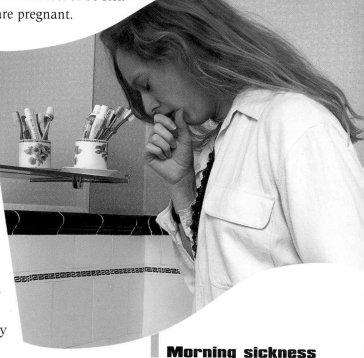

Morning sickness
In early pregnancy, a woman may feel or be sick.

The feelings that Gemma is experiencing could easily mean that she is pregnant. But it is important that she checks as soon as possible, so that she can work out what to do next.

The pregnancy test

A pregnancy test confirms whether someone is pregnant or not. The test works by checking whether the hormone HCG is present in the woman's urine. If no HCG is present, the result will be negative. If HCG is present, the result will be positive.

Pregnancy tests are very easy to perform. Most women organize their own. Tests involve either collecting a sample of urine in a clean container and dipping the test strip into it, or holding the test strip in the stream of urine as it is being passed. The urine passes along the test strip to two windows. If the test has worked properly, a coloured line or dot will appear in the smaller window. This is called the control. The test is positive if a coloured mark then appears also in the large window. This confirms the presence of HCG.

Pregnancy tests can be bought from the chemist, or can be organized for you at a family planning clinic, your GP surgery or a specialist clinic like those run by Brook (see page 60).

How long does pregnancy last?

The date that the baby is due is calculated from the date of the first day of the woman's last menstrual period. Pregnancy lasts 40 weeks from that date. Not all babies are born on exactly the calculated date, but 90 per cent deliver between one week before and one week after that date.

A positive test
A pink mark has appeared in the second window, showing the woman that she is pregnant.

2 Pregnancy
How the baby develops

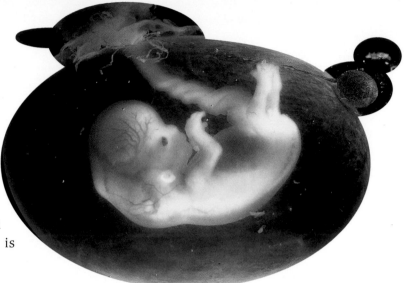

Pregnancy is amazing and wonderful. At conception, the female egg is fertilized by the male sperm, producing a single human cell. From this single human cell a human baby is formed.

How a cell becomes a baby

After fertilization in the Fallopian tube, the single cell starts to divide, making two cells, then four cells, then eight cells, then sixteen cells, and so on. This cell multiplication continues during the journey along the Fallopian tube to the uterus. By the time the one hundred-cell stage is reached, it is called an embryo and is ready to burrow (implant) itself into the lining of the uterus.

The embryo forms an attachment to the lining of the uterus, which will become the placenta. The placenta is a mass of blood vessels attached to the developing baby by the umbilical cord. The baby will gain oxygen and nutrients passed directly from its mother's blood via the placenta into its own blood, enabling it to grow.

Around the embryo, as it embeds in the lining of the womb, a sac starts to develop. This will become the fluid-filled amniotic sac. Whilst the baby grows and develops inside the uterus, it lies protected within the bag of amniotic fluid.

8-9 weeks old
At this stage the baby is about 17 mm long from head to bottom. It is floating in the amniotic sac and is attached to the placenta (top left) by the umbilical cord.

The first twelve weeks

Implantation takes place about two weeks after fertilization. However, pregnancy is normally calculated from the first day of the woman's last menstrual period. So implantation occurs about four weeks after that date. During the next eight weeks the baby will continue to develop from the 100-cell embryo. All the parts of the baby's body will be formed from these original identical cells. As the cellular embryo becomes a developing baby, it becomes known as a fetus.

The first parts of the baby to form are the brain and spinal cord and the heart. By six weeks, the baby's heart can be seen beating on an ultrasound scan (see page 20). The limbs start to develop, and then the features of the face – ears, eyes, mouth, etc. After development of the upper part of the limbs comes development of the feet and hands. At the same time, all the internal organs – heart, brain, lungs, kidneys, liver and gut – are continuing to form. By 12-14 weeks of pregnancy the baby is fully formed.

So you can understand that the greatest damage to a baby can occur during these first 12 weeks of pregnancy. Damage can be caused by a variety of external factors, such as drugs, alcohol and infections. Sometimes it is simply not possible to tell what has caused the damage. An abnormality caused by damage to the developing fetus is known as a congenital abnormality.

For example, if the heart does not develop normally, babies can be born with congenital heart disease. If development of the spinal cord is abnormal, spina bifida may result. If damage occurs at the time that the face is developing, it may not form normally and the baby may be born with a cleft of the lip and palate.

Thalidomide

In the early 1960s, a drug called thalidomide was commonly given to pregnant women to help treat pregnancy sickness. The drug damaged babies at the phase at which the limbs were developing. It caused major limb deformities.

The baby becomes viable

After 12-14 weeks, the fetus starts to grow fast. All the finer features of the baby start to form, such as eyebrows and eyelashes, fingernails and toenails. Between 16 and 18 weeks, the mother often starts to feel the baby moving in the womb. Initially it just feels like little flutterings but, as the weeks pass, the movements (kicks) get stronger.

From 24 weeks, the fetus is known as viable. This means that, if it were born at this stage, it is developed enough to have a chance of survival. It would obviously need intensive specialist care to survive, but all of the organs of the body are sufficiently well developed to make survival outside the womb a possibility. A baby born at this stage is still very immature. For example, the baby's eyes do not open until 26 weeks.

Intensive care
Prematurely born babies need intensive hospital care to enable them to develop and gain strength as they would have done in the mother's womb.

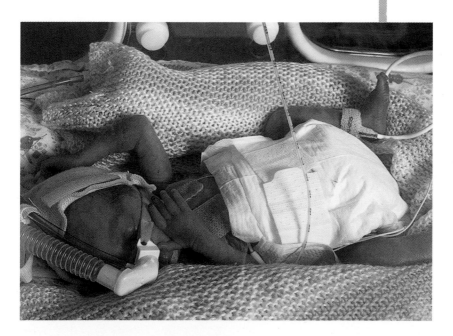

From about 32 weeks, the baby starts to settle into the position in the uterus from which it will be born. Most babies are born head first, but occasionally the baby settles into a position with its bottom downwards. If it is born in this position, it is called a breech delivery.

Pregnancy problems

During the early weeks, things can go so wrong that the pregnancy fails and miscarriage occurs. The woman notices bleeding from the vagina and will often then start to feel cramping abdominal pains. The doctor will probably arrange an ultrasound scan and, if it is not possible to see a beating fetal heart, then it is assumed that the fetus has died. Occasionally, the miscarriage will complete naturally – i.e. all the contents of the uterus are lost in the vaginal bleeding. Sometimes, to prevent excessive blood loss, the woman needs a brief operation to remove the contents of the uterus.

Sometimes the fertilized egg or embryo continues to grow in the Fallopian tube, instead of moving down and implanting in the uterus. This is known as an ectopic pregnancy and is potentially very dangerous for the mother. Past damage to the tube, and getting pregnant whilst using a coil for contraception, increase the risk of an ectopic pregnancy.

Antenatal care

This is the care given to women during pregnancy. (Antenatal means 'before birth'.) The aim of antenatal care is to ensure that the mother remains healthy throughout pregnancy and that the baby develops normally. In the past, pregnancy was a dangerous time for women. Many women died from the complications of pregnancy, and the risks to the baby were also high. This remains the case in the developing world today. In the developed world, with better health and nutrition and improved care during pregnancy, the risks have reduced dramatically.

Declining death rates

The number of deaths per thousand babies born in England declined from 62 to 8 between 1930 and 1995. The decline is an example of how pregnancy and birth have become safer in the developed world.

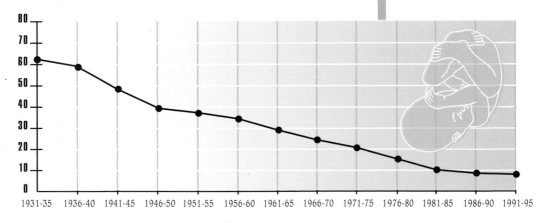

A number of professionals share the care of women during pregnancy. Midwives are nurses specially trained to look after pregnant women antenatally, during delivery, and for a short time after the birth (postnatally). The family doctor will also participate in this care and will continue to look after mother and baby after birth. Obstetricians are doctors who specialize in looking after pregnancy. They become involved when complications arise during pregnancy or delivery.

Care during the first half of pregnancy is directed to helping the mother decide where she wants to have her baby – in hospital or at home – and then to helping her decide about antenatal tests to look for abnormalities in the baby. There is never any compulsion to have tests, nor to terminate the pregnancy if the baby is found to have a problem.

Antenatal tests

Antenatal tests look for babies affected by Down's syndrome, spina bifida and other structural abnormalities. If abnormalities are found, couples can be offered termination of pregnancy.

Women can be offered blood tests or special types of scan, to check the risk of their baby being affected. If the risk is found to be very high, then other tests, such as amniocentesis, can be offered, to confirm whether the baby is affected. Amniocentesis involves passing a needle into the amniotic fluid in the uterus, withdrawing some fluid and then testing it.

A worrying decision

Jo and Ann are expecting their first baby. They have been offered tests to see if their baby might be suffering from Down's syndrome or spina bifida. Ann had a blood test done at 16 weeks pregnant and she has just found out that the test is positive. She knows that this means that her baby has a higher chance of being affected by one of these problems, but the only way she can be certain is by having an amniocentesis. She is very frightened about this. She knows there is a possibility that she will have a miscarriage just because the test involves putting a needle into the amniotic sac. She doesn't like needles and is scared for her baby. She is also very nervous about finding out the result of the test. She and Jo are still uncertain about whether they would want to terminate the pregnancy if the test shows that the baby is affected. It is a very worrying time for them.

A midwife describes her work

When I first meet a woman at the start of her pregnancy, I explain about the care she will have. There are blood tests to arrange to make sure that she is healthy. She then has important decisions to make about whether she wants to have tests done to check that her developing baby is normal. I tell her that the tests are available in the first half of pregnancy and that, if she finds that her baby is affected, it would be possible to offer an abortion. I must also tell her about ultrasound scans. These are a safe way of looking at the baby during pregnancy. Later in the pregnancy I will see the woman more often to check her own health and that the baby is growing well.

It's also my job to prepare women for childbirth and the arrival of their new baby. I do this with individual women and in classes. We discuss feelings about pregnancy, how to feed the baby, what you need when the baby arrives, and all sorts of other useful things.

When a woman goes into labour, I'm there to look after her, to check that she stays well and that the baby's heartbeat is healthy despite the stress of labour. Then the really exciting part starts when I guide the woman through the process of delivering her baby into the world. The baby's first cry and the woman's relief at the end of labour are really moving.

Listening in
The midwife can check the baby's heartbeat by listening through a simple funnel.

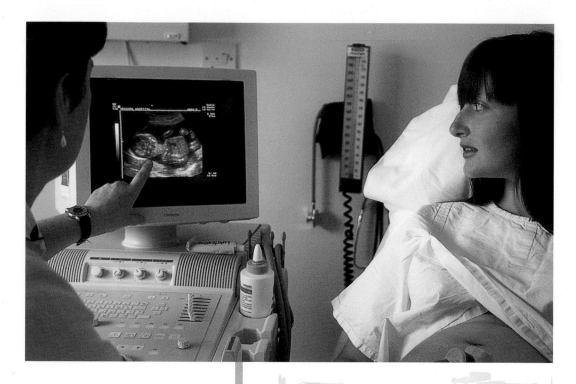

Having a scan

Some warmed gel rubbed on the woman's stomach helps the scanning instrument to make good contact and get a clear picture of inside the uterus.

In the second half of pregnancy, the aim of antenatal care is to check that the woman stays well. This involves picking up any pregnancy-related problems such as high blood pressure. The health of the growing baby is also monitored. The size of the uterus is checked to make sure the baby is growing, the baby's heart is listened to, and the mother is asked how lively the baby is in the uterus. Monitoring the baby's kicks is a good way of knowing that it is healthy.

The ultrasound scan

An ultrasound scan is a test using soundwaves to build up an image of the baby in the uterus. The test is safe to mother and baby, and research continues to check the safety of the test.

The test

- *checks measurements and growth of the baby*
- *checks whether there is more than one baby in the uterus*
- *detects abnormalities of parts of the baby, e.g. the face and spine*
- *shows the position of the placenta*

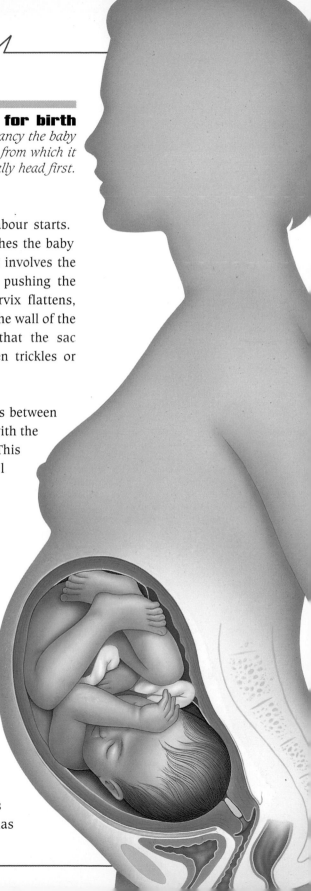

*At the end of pregnancy the baby
settles into the position from which it
will be be born – usually head first.*

Delivery

When it is time for the baby to be born, labour starts.
Labour is the means by which the body pushes the baby
out of the uterus and through the vagina. It involves the
muscle wall of the uterus contracting and pushing the
baby downwards. The long tube of the cervix flattens,
thins, then stretches open. The membranes (the wall of the
amniotic sac) often rupture. This means that the sac
bursts and the fluid that was inside it then trickles or
gushes from the vagina.

For the vast majority of women, labour starts between
39 and 41 weeks pregnant. It usually starts with the
onset of regular and painful contractions. This
means that the woman feels painful
tightenings of the uterus, followed by
periods of relaxation. The contractions
become stronger and more frequent as
labour progresses. Labour lasts, on average,
between six and twelve hours.

When the cervix has dilated fully, the
woman gets the urge to push. The
midwife preparing to deliver the baby
will instruct the woman about how to
push carefully to avoid the baby being
born too quickly or too slowly. This
allows the skin and muscles around the
vagina to stretch gradually, thereby
avoiding them tearing during delivery.

Once the baby's head has been born, the
body follows quickly and easily. As soon as
the baby is born, the umbilical cord which has

attached the baby to the placenta is clamped and cut. The baby is then passed to its mother to cuddle. She may also wish to put the baby to the breast for a first feed.

Sometimes the baby is a little slow taking its first breath and may need some help. The nose and mouth are sucked out and the baby can be given some oxygen.

After the birth of the baby, the placenta (sometimes known as the after-birth) must be delivered.

Difficulties with labour

Sometimes labour does not start at the right time. If the woman has not started labour within a week or two after her due date, then labour is induced by giving drugs to stimulate the uterus to contract. If problems occur during pregnancy, such as poor growth of the baby, then labour may be induced early.

Sometimes, at the end of labour, the contractions are not strong enough to push the baby out. It can be helped by using forceps or Ventouse (a vacuum extraction device). These are applied to the baby's head and the obstetrician then pulls the baby out.

Sometimes the obstetrician recommends that the baby should be born by Caesarian section. This is an operation where a cut is made through the skin of the abdomen and then through the muscle of the uterus and the baby is delivered through the opening. The operation is sometimes planned, or may be needed as an emergency during labour if things are not progressing normally.

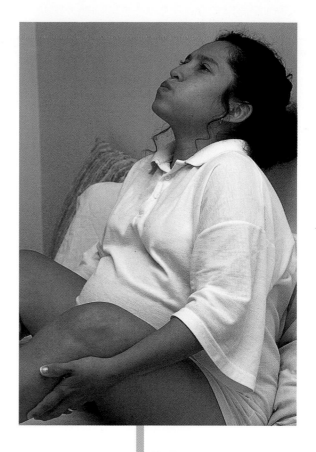

Labour
Breathing exercises help make the pain of labour easier to cope with. Pregnant women are taught these exercises as part of their antenatal care.

Postnatal care

During the first few days after delivery, the new mother must recover from the physical stress of labour and get to know her new baby. She is confronted with many experiences for the first time. Most importantly, she must learn how to feed her baby.

During the first few days after delivery, blood is lost from the vagina as the area where the placenta was attached starts to heal. The uterus contracts from its large size (extending up to the woman's ribs at the end of pregnancy) to its normal size (about the size of a small orange).

The woman is very tired after the physical stress of labour, and the baby is also making many physical and emotional demands. Many women (about 80 per cent) experience the 'baby blues'. At around the third or fourth day after delivery they feel very low and weepy and are easily upset. These feelings usually resolve quickly, helped by the support of the woman's partner and family and the professionals. However, for about 10 per cent of women, the feelings continue and coping with the baby becomes very difficult. This is known as postnatal depression. The causes of it are not fully understood, but midwives, family doctors and health visitors are very aware of the problem and offer support and treatment for women who become depressed.

The woman, her partner and the baby are now a new family and are starting on the pleasures, excitement, trials and tribulations of family life for many years to come!

A family
A baby brings fun and excitement as well as constant work!

3 Look after yourself!
Protecting your fertility

The way you live can affect your ability to get pregnant in the future and to carry a pregnancy successfully. The influence of lifestyle on fertility applies to both women and men.

For males, sperm production can be reduced by excessive alcohol consumption, by cigarette smoking, and by recreational drug use. Anabolic steroids, which are used illegally by some athletes to enhance their performance, also suppress sperm production. Similarly, some treatments prescribed by doctors (for instance, for cancer) can reduce the number of sperm produced. Some men are exposed to toxins in their work place that may adversely affect their future fertility.

Sperm production can also be affected by damage to the testis. Damage can occur by physical injury – for example, falling astride the crossbar of a bike, causing trauma to the testes. Equally, damage can be caused by some infections. The most notable of these is mumps, where the mumps virus infects the testes.

For females, using recreational drugs, smoking to excess, and being obese are all factors that can result in reduced fertility. This means that it can be more difficult to get

Alcohol
Drinking alcohol might seem a 'macho' thing to do, but drinking to excess can lead to a reduced sperm count.

pregnant when you want to. There are circumstances in women's lives that stop the ovarian cycle working normally, thereby stopping ovulation and periods. Many girls with eating disorders who lose excessive amounts of weight find that their periods stop. Similarly, girls training as professional athletes may find that the rigors of the training programme halt their ovarian cycle and periods stop.

'I've just got engaged and when we're married, I'd really love us to have kids. I just hope that all the stress when I was a teenager hasn't affected my chances. I got anorexic and my weight fell to about five stone, and I don't think I had any periods for two or three years.'
(Kathryn, aged 25)

The use of alcohol and drugs can lead to other behaviours that put young people at risk. Alcohol and drugs can reduce inhibitions and lead people more easily into casual sexual relationships. This then increases their risk of catching a sexually transmitted infection (STI).

Recreational drug use is illegal and expensive. To raise the funds to maintain their drug habit, some young people of both sexes become involved in prostitution – so putting themselves at risk of infection and pregnancy.

Sexually transmitted infections

The commonest cause of infertility, in women, is blockage of the Fallopian tubes (the route that the egg has to take from the ovary to the uterus). Infection is the most common cause of this blockage, and the infection most often involved is chlamydia.

Chlamydia is not just a female problem. Chlamydial infection in men can reduce the activity levels of sperm, thereby reducing the chances of their being able to fertilize the egg. The difficulty with chlamydia is that the majority of men and women who catch the infection are unaware of any problem until the damage is done. Chlamydial infection is common particularly in young people who are sexually active. Various studies from Western Europe have shown that up to 20 per cent of women aged 15-19 years may be infected.

Gonorrhoea

Gonorrhoea is another STI which can cause similar problems to chlamydia. The people most at increased risk are the young sexually active. The diagnosis of gonorrhoea has increased by 50 per cent in men aged 16 to 19 and by 40 per cent in women of the same age, in some centres in Europe.

Lucy's test results

Hi, I'm Lucy. I've just had a real shock. Lee, my boyfriend, told me last week that he had these spots on his penis. He'd seen his doctor and he's been told he's got warts. He also said he had to tell me, because I ought to have a check-up. I psyched myself up to go to one of those clinics that deal with sexually transmitted infections. I found an advice number in one of my magazines and they told me how to organize it. So I've been. I didn't enjoy the experience, but I suppose they were OK. The bad news is that the swab for chlamydia came back positive, so I've had to have treatment. They took my first smear test. They told me that we all have to have those and they check for cancer of the cervix. What's even worse is that they have found wart virus in that smear, so I'll have to keep having that repeated to check.

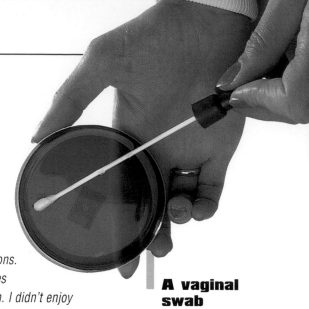

A vaginal swab

AIDS

This baby with AIDS was born in Cambodia, a country with a very high rate of HIV infection.

Unfortunately, STIs don't occur in isolation. People with one infection are likely to have other infections too. The other serious infections that can be acquired at the same time are hepatitis B and the HIV virus. These are both transmitted sexually. People usually do not know that they have caught the infection until many months or even years later. Many people who catch one of these viruses will become life-long carriers of it. It will never leave their body. As most people do not know they are carriers, unless they have had special blood tests to prove it, they continue to spread the virus to other people by unprotected sexual contact. Women carriers can pass the virus to their baby when they are pregnant. Up to 25 per cent of babies born to HIV-positive mothers are born infected by the virus and are unlikely to survive until adulthood.

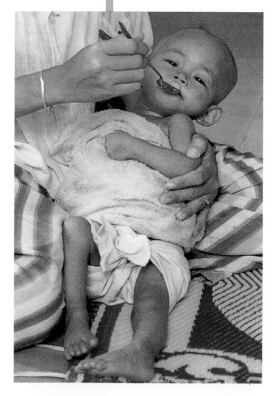

Positive thinking

On a more positive note, what can couples do, when they are thinking about planning a pregnancy, in order to look after themselves and their baby? In order to enhance their chances of getting pregnant, and of having a healthy pregnancy, women are advised to:

- stop smoking
- reduce their alcohol consumption
- aim for their ideal weight
- check that their rubella (German measles) immunity is adequate
- take extra folic acid (both before getting pregnant and for the first 12 weeks of pregnancy).

Rubella
A new-born baby with congenital rubella syndrome.

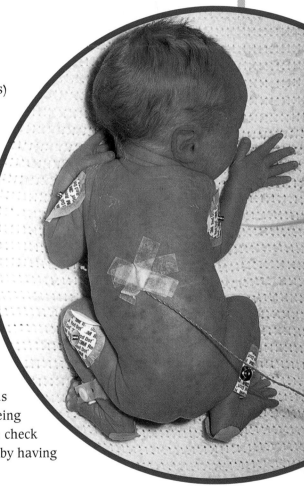

Rubella is a children's infectious disease causing a rash and fever for a few days. But, if a pregnant woman catches rubella in the early weeks of pregnancy, her baby is very likely to be born with the congenital rubella syndrome. Babies affected by this suffer from deafness, blindness, heart abnormalities and mental handicap. Immunization against rubella (which prevents you from catching it) has dramatically reduced the chance of babies being born with this syndrome. Young women can check that their immunization has been successful by having a blood test.

Taking extra folic acid (one of the B vitamins) helps prevent babies being born with neural tube defects. The most common of these is spina bifida, when the baby is born with a section of the spinal cord in the low back exposed. The cord becomes damaged, leaving the child paralysed from the waist down.

A high risk of pregnancy

Danielle (16) and Tony (18) have both left school but are not in regular jobs. They have been going out together for six months. They go to clubs in town and have a good time drinking and dancing. Drugs are readily available if you know who to talk to and you have the ready cash. Danielle knows that Tony and his mates break into cars and steal the radio equipment. It is easy to sell this on. So Tony usually does have ready cash for cannabis or ecstasy. During the day, life is pretty boring. They occasionally have casual work in the supermarket. But, to pass the time, they both smoke about 20 cigarettes per day. They started having sex early in their relationship. Danielle is on the pill, but often forgets to take it. Tony refuses to use condoms. They have both had sexual partners before. Tony had sex with men when he was younger. He was already into drugs when he was 15 and an older man found him partners who would pay him for sex. Danielle is at high risk of getting pregnant. The lifestyle that she and Tony lead will be very likely to damage their baby.

Smoking during pregnancy

When you smoke, nicotine and carbon monoxide get into your blood. This reduces the supply of oxygen to your baby and stops it growing well.

Why avoid smoking, alcohol and drugs?

It is well known that smoking whilst pregnant causes problems. The baby will not grow so well in the uterus and there is also a much higher chance that the baby will be born prematurely (too early). The risks to a baby are greater if it is both underweight and premature.

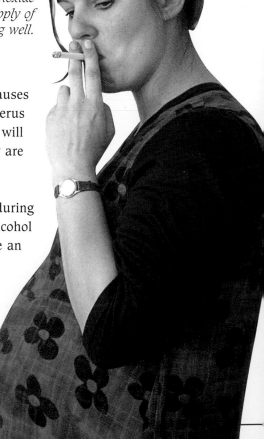

If a woman consumes a large volume of alcohol during pregnancy, her baby can be born with the fetal alcohol syndrome. Babies with this problem are small, have an odd facial appearance, and fail to develop normally.

Cannabis used during pregnancy does not seem to affect the growth of the baby. However, there is evidence that when these babies are toddlers, they perform less well than those whose mothers did not use cannabis in pregnancy.

If a pregnant woman uses heroin, it crosses the placenta and affects the baby. Some days after birth, these babies experience withdrawal effects from the heroin they have been used to. They become irritable and have difficulties with breathing and feeding. They are effectively heroin addicts at birth. During the period of withdrawal the baby is often very ill and may need intensive care.

Infections

Infections caught by a mother during pregnancy can upset the well-being of the baby in the uterus.

- Infections caught from other people (e.g. chicken pox or German measles) can infect the baby, causing damage to it.
- Infections caught from animals can harm the baby. The organism Toxoplasma is found in the faeces of cats. If this infection is caught by a woman during pregnancy, it can seriously damage the fetus. Sheep can themselves miscarry or give birth to sick lambs after infection with an organism called Listeria. If a woman handles infected sheep during lambing, she too can miscarry.
- Infections can be caught from the food that we eat. Toxoplasma can be found in raw meat. Salmonella is found in raw eggs. Listeria is often found in soft cheeses such as Brie and blue cheeses, pâté and cooked-chilled meals. To avoid infection, it is very important that such meals are properly reheated.
- Sexually transmitted infections such as hepatitis B and HIV can be transmitted direct to the baby in the uterus, and the baby will be born infected by the virus.

Heroin
In the UK half of all people under 35 yrs have experimented with drugs, one third are regular drug users and 3 per cent have a drug problem. Heroin use is increasingly common in people aged under 25 years.

4 Teenage pregnancy
Figures and facts

Why do teenagers get pregnant?

Many studies about teenage pregnancy and parenthood have been performed in both Europe and the USA. It seems that most teenage pregnancies are unplanned, perhaps as many as 75 per cent of them. But there are variations. For example, among some ethnic groups, it is the accepted norm to marry and start a family before you are 20.

Certain factors make it more likely that you will be one of those young girls who finds herself pregnant, or a young man who becomes a father, as a teenager. However,

Births per 1,000 women aged 15–19
The UK has the highest rate of teenage births in Western Europe.

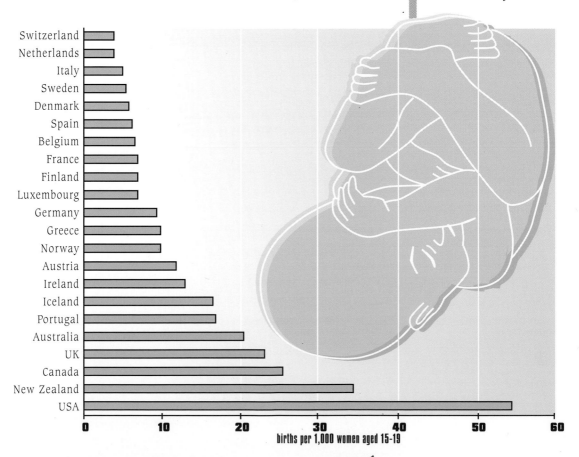

births per 1,000 women aged 15-19

pregnancy can still happen to anyone who is sexually active.

Children whose own mother was a teenager when they were born are more likely to have babies as teenagers themselves. It seems that teenagers who have left school early or are excluded from education are more likely to get pregnant. Teenagers who are poor and socially disadvantaged see little future for themselves other than early relationships and are therefore more likely to get pregnant. Conversely, young people who see a good future for themselves in terms of further education and employment are more likely to make sure that they have enough information about pregnancy and contraception to avoid pregnancy until they are ready.

Teenagers who have been sexually abused are very likely to become pregnant while still very young. Mental health problems in adolescence contribute to low self-esteem and confidence. It seems that this can lead young people into unprotected and inappropriate relationships and consequently the possibility of pregnancy. But remember that unprotected sex, whatever the circumstance, can result in pregnancy.

International variations

The rate of teenage pregnancy varies widely from country to country. There have also been large differences over time between countries. In Denmark, the number of births to women aged 15-19 has declined steeply from 40 per 1,000 in 1966 to well under 10 per 1,000 since the early 1980s. In the USA, the number of births to women aged 15-19 started to rise in the late 1980s and peaked at over 60 per 1,000 in 1991. Why is there such a difference between

Getting pregnant – the truth

You may hear some myths about things that help avoid pregnancy. Myths are not true! The facts are:

1. *It is easy to get pregnant the first time you have sex.*

2. *Of teenagers who have unprotected sex, 90 per cent of them will be pregnant within a year of starting the relationship.*

3. *Girls can still get pregnant when they think they are menstruating (having a period).*

4. *You can get pregnant if you have sex standing up.*

5. *Girls do not have to have an orgasm to get pregnant.*

6. *If the boy pulls his penis out of the vagina just before he ejaculates, it is still possible to get pregnant. Some sperm may have been released into the vagina before ejaculation.*

7. *It can also be possible to get pregnant even if the boy ejaculates outside but very close to the vagina. Sperm are strong swimmers!*

countries that in many ways are very similar? It seems that the countries that have been most successful in lowering the rate of teenage pregnancy have some characteristics in common:

- good sex education in schools, so that young people learn fact and not myth and learn about sex in the context of relationships
- good facilities for contraception, including easy access for teenagers
- teenagers are happy to delay the start of sexual activity because they feel strong and assertive about relationships
- good education and job prospects for young people
- family attitudes to discussing sex are open. Teenagers find it easy to talk to their parents and family members about their relationships.

UK figures

In the UK in 1998 there were 100,000 pregnancies in girls aged 15-19 years. There were 8,400 pregnancies in girls under 16 years.

Roughly 50 per cent of pregnant teenagers under 16 years opt for abortion.

Roughly 33 per cent of pregnant teenagers aged 16 and 17 years opt for abortion.

A baby is for keeps

Mary-Jo and Craig are both 14 when Mary-Jo discovers that she is pregnant. If they are a mature pair and are able to talk about their relationship and the meaning of this unexpected pregnancy, there are a lot of things that they will need to consider. The end result of pregnancy is the arrival of a baby. What does that mean in reality? Babies have many needs, including:

Love and affection, ideally from both parents

Will Craig stay around throughout Mary-Jo's pregnancy, even though she will not always be able to go out with him? Will he be there in hospital when the baby is born? Will Mary-Jo and Craig together be able to give the love that the baby will need all through childhood? After all, it will start school before they are 20.

Feeding. Breastfeeding is the safest and healthiest way to feed babies. It helps protect them from infections and ill-health through childhood.

How will Mary-Jo feel about feeding her baby? How will Craig support her? Babies need feeding during the night as well as the day. How will they cope with getting up in the night for feeds?

To be kept dry and clean. Babies have no control over their bowels or bladder. Their skin is very sensitive. If it is left in contact with urine or faeces, it will become red and sore. In order to prevent this, babies need regular changing of their nappies. Most people nowadays in Europe and the USA use disposable nappies. The alternative is terry nappies that can be washed and re-used.

Newborn babies may need 6 or 10 clean nappies every day! Will Craig and Mary-Jo be able to make nappy-changing time fun and a time to get to know their baby? How will they afford to buy the endless supply of new nappies that they will need?

Care. Babies and then children are dependent on their parents for all their needs until they themselves are adults. These needs include a warm, safe home, clothing, food and education. They cannot be left unattended.

How will Craig and Mary-Jo feel about the restriction that their baby will impose on their social life? It will not be easy for them to go out together after the baby is born. Meanwhile, their friends will still be going to discos and having a good time.

Attention when it cries. Newborn babies are able to do very little other than sleep, feed and cry. It can be very difficult to work out why a baby is crying. The list of possible reasons is endless. The baby may be hungry. It may be uncomfortable because it has a wet or dirty nappy. It may be too hot or too cold. It may have wind or colic. It may be tired but unable to sleep. It may be bored and wanting to play or lonely and wanting company.

What's wrong?
Babies and very young children cannot tell us what is upsetting them.

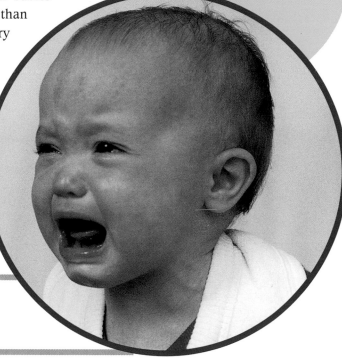

What will Craig and Mary-Jo feel like when their baby cries and won't stop? How will they manage?

Attention when it is ill. Babies and young children are often ill. They easily catch infections from other young children. It can be very frightening when your child suddenly becomes sick.

How will Mary-Jo and Craig cope in this situation? Will they know how to get help?

Is being pregnant as a teenager good for you?

There are risks attached to being pregnant at any age, but the risks are greater when very young or at the end of reproductive life. Pregnancy problems are more common in teenage pregnancies. These include high blood pressure and the risk of a dangerous illness called eclampsia. Prolonged or difficult labour is more common, particularly in girls who are not fully grown when they get pregnant.

Teenagers are the group most likely to smoke in pregnancy. Of teenagers who are pregnant, two thirds have smoked before getting pregnant and 50 per cent continue to smoke through the pregnancy. We have already seen the harmful effects of smoking in pregnancy (page 28).

As most teenagers have not planned to be pregnant, few have taken health measures before conceiving and at the very start of pregnancy. For example, very few are taking folic acid supplements (see page 27).

As soon as you know you are pregnant, you must think about whether you want to continue with the pregnancy or choose termination or adoption. You must cope with the idea of being pregnant and consider how to tell your family and friends. If you decide to keep the baby, you must start preparing for parenthood. Many teenagers faced with these dilemmas end up delaying the decisions. Their pregnancy is therefore confirmed much later than in an older woman who is keen to be pregnant. The delays are often the result of not expecting to be pregnant, fear of disapproval, fear that your privacy will not be respected, fear that everyone will tell you to have an abortion, or simply wanting to deny that it is happening to you. As a result, a high proportion of pregnant teenagers do not see their family doctor early in pregnancy and do not have early antenatal care.

Looking ahead
Samantha feels proud to be pregnant. But what will life hold for her and and her baby?

Depression

Postnatal depression (see page 23) is three times more common after giving birth whilst still a teenager. Four out of every ten young mothers will be affected.

Social problems

Teenage parents are more likely than their peers to live in poverty and be unemployed. Their chances in life are also poorer. People who have been teenage parents are less likely to be in well-paid jobs, even when they have reached their thirties. Teenage parents are less likely to complete their education and training.

Relationships that start when you are a teenager have a higher chance of breaking down than relationships when you are older. In a British study, 50 per cent of teenage mothers were no longer with the father of their baby one year after the baby's birth. Having a baby puts an extra stress on a relationship.

Teenagers worry about their housing when they get pregnant. Some are lucky to have supportive families who either let them stay in the family home with their baby or help them to live elsewhere. Other teenage parents have trouble finding accommodation that they can afford.

Being a parent while still a young teenager does restrict your social life. Before you go out, you must always think first about how to care for your baby.

But the story does not always have to be one of doom and gloom. There are teenagers, like Cath, who become excellent parents, who get the support of their families and manage to complete their education and find good jobs.

Children of teenage parents

Babies of teenage mothers are 25 per cent more likely than those of older mothers to weigh under 2.5 kg at birth. Being small at birth carries risks to health and well-being.

Death rates for babies of teenage mothers are 60 per cent higher than for babies of older mothers.

Death rates for children aged 1-3 years are highest if their mother is under 20 years old.

Children of very young parents are more likely to suffer accidents during early childhood.

These young children are twice as likely to be admitted to hospital after an accident or with an illness as children of older mothers.

Cath and Amy

Hi, I'm Cath. I'm 16 now but I had my daughter Amy when I was 13. I was dead scared when I thought I was pregnant and didn't know what Mum and Dad would say. I knew they would be really disappointed with me. I decided just to keep quiet, but still no period came. About 6 months later, Mum noticed my swollen tummy. She frog-marched me to the doctor who sent me for a scan. And there was **my** baby. I didn't know whether to shout for joy or cry. Mum was with me and although she was really upset that I'd been so silly, she stuck with me and talked Dad round. When I went into labour, Mum came with me too. I didn't know anything could be so painful and scary, so I screamed and held on to Mum. After ten hours and with the help of forceps, Amy was born and she was just perfect. It was love at first sight.

Homework
As well as keeping up with her school work, Cath has started to read and write with Amy.

Coming home and those first weeks were tough. Mum and Dad were great, but I was so tired, getting up at night and all. Some of my friends thought it was great. Others didn't want to know. They were all still doing their own thing, going shopping, having sleepovers, and I couldn't join in.

Getting back to school was the hardest part. I'm lucky because my family mind Amy while I'm at school so I can go back to where I was before and be with my friends there. Doing homework, making Amy's tea, getting her bathed and ready for bed is all really exhausting, but I still love her to bits. Everything's working out because my family have been so great.

You notice that Amy's Dad doesn't feature much. He left me when I was pregnant. He's dead chuffed to be a Dad and sees Amy some weekends, but he's only 16 now and he has a new girlfriend. I'm determined to make something of myself. It's big exams this year. I wish I hadn't got pregnant so young, but then I wouldn't have Amy and she's gorgeous.

Sex education – the facts

Good sex education in school, from family and from other sources helps teenagers to make informed decisions. There have been many programmes around the world to help young people understand their sexuality. The more they understand their feelings, the more able they are to make rational decisions about when to start having a sexual relationship and how to use contraception and protection against sexually transmitted infection.

In the Netherlands, for example, sex education is an important part of the school programme. It includes not just scientific descriptions of the biology of sex, but also work on morality and ethics. When asked, Dutch teenagers report far fewer inhibitions about talking to their parents about sex and relationships than teenagers in the UK. Contraception is free and easily available to teenagers in a confidential environment. 85 per cent of teenagers use contraception at first intercourse in the Netherlands, compared with 50 per cent in the UK, 78 per cent in the USA and 80 per cent in Denmark.

Changing styles

Schools have always taught the biology of sex and reproduction. In 1948 (above) it was remarkable for a class to be able to see a film on the subject. Today, some schools have programmable computer babies, to help students learn aspects of child-care.

As a result of their sex education, Dutch teenagers have one of the lowest rates of conception in the world. They also, on average, delay the start of sexual relationships to an older age. Young men in the Netherlands are more likely to discuss contraception with their girlfriends.

Other programmes have been developed in Britain and the USA, particularly in areas of high rates of teenage pregnancy. Some programmes use young people to teach others a similar age to themselves. An example is 'Teen advocates', attached to the Bronx Center for Planned Parenthood in New York. Young people are trained to teach others. They use a drama programme to engage their audience in discussion. Being the same age and from the same place, they use language and examples that teenagers can relate to. It seems that teenagers who have seen the presentations are more able to make decisions about their own sexual health and discuss contraception and other related topics.

'I thought sex ed at school would be terrible. But we had these cool sessions with older kids leading them. I don't feel so hung up about talking about sex and contraception now.'

A programme used in schools in Devon in the UK covers awareness of relationships and attitudes to others and information about sexual relationships and contraception. It is taught partly by teachers and school nurses but, from the age of 14, students are also taught by other teenagers aged 16-19, who have been through the programme themselves. Most students say that they have gained both skills and useful information from the sessions and feel that their sex education has been acceptable.

So, being informed helps you to feel confident in your relationships. This self-confidence helps you to make the choice about when you start having sex. It means that you are more likely to use reliable contraception when you do have sex. It means that young men are more likely to use condoms to protect against sexually transmitted infection.

5 Unwanted pregnancy
Looking at the options

Ann's dilemma

Ann, aged 16, has been getting worried. Her period is late and she feels sick. She doesn't know much about pregnancy, but she has heard her Mum chatting with a neighbour, who felt terrible at the beginning of pregnancy. She has read in her magazines about girls getting pregnant. She doesn't really think that she could be pregnant. She and her boyfriend Nick have only had sex a few times. But neither of them has done much about contraception. Ann had been thinking of asking her friend about how she got the pill.

Pregnancy is not always a straightforward happy event. Many women get pregnant accidentally. For some women, and for most young teenagers, who have not planned to have a baby, the discovery that they are pregnant is frightening. The first thing they need to do is talk to someone professional, such as their GP or a family planning clinic.

Adoption

Adoption used to be a very common choice for unmarried women who found themselves pregnant. For example, in England and Wales in 1975 there were about 21,000 adoptions. By 1996, this number had fallen to around 6,000. It is likely that the fall in numbers of adoptions is related to the wider availability of contraception, but also importantly to the wider availability of abortion.

If Ann is pregnant, what are her options?

- She can continue with her pregnancy and look after her baby with Nick's help, or on her own, or with the help of her family.
- She can continue with her pregnancy but, when the baby is born, arrange to give the baby up for adoption.
- She can arrange to have an abortion (termination).

What is an abortion?

The word abortion actually means ending of pregnancy so that it does not result in the birth of a child. Abortion can occur naturally. This is known as miscarriage or spontaneous abortion. An induced or therapeutic abortion is done on purpose to end a pregnancy.

About 90 per cent of abortions are performed during the first 12 weeks of pregnancy. Abortion to end an unwanted pregnancy is common. It is estimated that 1 in every 3 women will have had an abortion during their lives.

Abortion can be done by one of three methods:

Medical abortion can only be performed before 9 weeks of pregnancy, by a specialist abortion clinic. A drug called mifepristone is given; then 48 hours later, a drug called prostaglandin is given as a tablet into the vagina. Usually within four hours bleeding starts from the vagina, accompanied by some cramping pain. The blood contains the contents of the uterus – i.e. the very early pregnancy.

Seeking advice
It's important to seek advice as soon as you think you might be pregnant.

The UK law on abortion

*In the UK, termination of pregnancy is not available on demand, but it **is** readily available. The law for England, Scotland and Wales states that, to allow abortion, two doctors must certify that:*

A *continuing the pregnancy would involve risk to the life of the pregnant woman greater than if the pregnancy were terminated*

B *terminating the pregnancy is necessary to prevent grave, permanent injury to the physical or mental health of the pregnant woman*

C *the pregnancy has NOT exceeded its 24th week and continuing it would involve risk, greater than if it were terminated, of injury to the physical or mental health of the pregnant woman*

D *the pregnancy has NOT exceeded its 24th week and continuing it would involve risk, greater than if it were terminated, of injury to the physical or mental health of any existing child(ren) of the family of the pregnant woman*

E *there is substantial risk that if the child were born it would suffer from such physical or mental abnormalities as to be seriously handicapped.*

Suction termination of pregnancy, or **vacuum extraction**, is by far the most common form of abortion. It can be done between 6 and 13 weeks of pregnancy, and must be performed in a specialist clinic or a hospital. It is an operation done under local or general anaesthetic and lasting 5-15 minutes. The cervix is stretched a little to allow a suction tube to be passed through it and into the uterus. The contents of the uterus (i.e. the early pregnancy) are sucked out. Most women recover quickly and go home the same day.

Rights and wrongs
Many people have strong feelings about the ethics of abortion. This woman demonstrated against a law which would make abortion illegal. She believed that such a law would deny women's freedom and right to choose.

Later abortions are done after 13 weeks of pregnancy and are uncommon. Either they are performed by using prostaglandin in the vagina, to make the uterus contract and expel the pregnancy, or, occasionally, a surgical termination is performed. This involves stretching the cervix under general anaesthetic and removing the contents of the uterus in fragments, using instruments.

Is it killing?
Many people argue that abortion is an illegal killing.

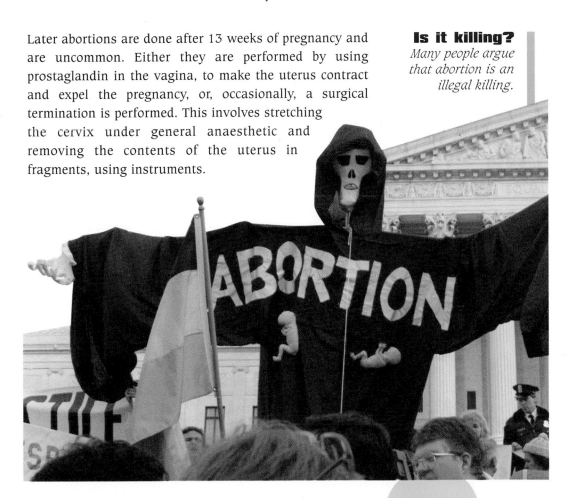

Answers to Ann's questions

Ann thinks that abortion might be the solution for her and Nick, but she has a lot of questions:

- Will she be able to become pregnant in the future? If the abortion goes smoothly, there is no risk to her future ability to conceive.
- Will it hurt? The operation is not painful, but is often followed by period-like pain and bleeding for a few days.
- Will anyone else know about the operation? Ann will receive totally confidential care.
- Will the fetus feel pain? There is no scientific evidence that the fetus at less than 26 weeks is able to feel.

Things are not always as easy and as organized as this sounds. Finding themselves pregnant and not knowing about the services available, women react in differing ways.

Some young women enter a phase of denial about being pregnant. They have heard that periods can stop if you feel under pressure or have lost a lot of weight. The idea of talking to a strange professional person or to their parents about the possibility of being pregnant is much too difficult. Denying their pregnancy means that they continue without any antenatal care and eventually go in to labour and give birth with no preparation.

Other women deliberately hide their pregnancy. They make a decision to move away from their home area and proceed with the pregnancy in privacy. Sometimes they are very organized, seek professional help, have antenatal care, deliver the baby safely and then hand it over for adoption. They can then return home as though nothing had happened. They do, however, remain weighed down by the burden of their secrecy.

Sometimes, having concealed their pregnancy, women are still too anxious to seek professional help. They give birth to their baby out of hospital and with no assistance. In this case the young woman is totally unprepared for motherhood and looking after a new baby. The desperation of the situation can lead her to extremes of behaviour. It is not uncommon for women like this to abandon their babies. The mother often does her best to look after the baby by wrapping it carefully and leaving it in a place where it will inevitably be found.

Paper-boy finds baby under bush

A PAPER-BOY found a new-born baby abandoned under a bush in freezing weather as he cycled home from his Boxing Day round.

Mother of abandoned baby says 'I want her to have a special life'

Babies find haven in 'postbox'

A BAPTIST minister has built a steel 'delivery box' into a wall of her Johannesburg church to tackle a growing crisis of abandoned babies in South Africa. Unwanted infants can now be 'posted' there by their mothers rather than being left to die in places such as dustbins or down drains. In the first three months, 13 babies have been delivered through this 'Door of Hope'.

Germans 'post' unwanted babies

A BABY-BANK where mothers can safely abandon unwanted infants by pushing them through a hatch into the care of social workers is to open in Germany.

Sadly, a young mother's desperation about how to cope after giving birth may drive her to kill her own baby. Infanticide is defined as the killing of newborn infants by their parents. It is estimated that one baby is killed every day in the USA. Studies performed in the USA suggest that people most likely to kill their babies shortly after giving birth are young teenage mothers under 15 years old, girls under 19 years old who already have a child, and girls who have opted out of education at a young age. They have usually concealed their pregnancy and have not had antenatal care. Some of the girls who find themselves in this situation have conceived as a result of sexual abuse.

Infanticide

Studies in the UK have shown that 9 out of every 200,000 babies are killed by their parents. 21 per cent of those are killed on their first day of life and usually by their mother. However, those babies who are killed after the first day are as likely to be killed by their father as by their mother.

Mothers who kill their babies in the very early days after giving birth have often become depressed and are finding it difficult to cope with the needs of their baby. About 10 per cent of women become seriously depressed after childbirth (postnatal depression). The babies of depressed women are more irritable and less easily consoled. The combination of maternal depression and an unsettled baby makes it more likely that the baby will be harmed.

Depression

Mothers with postnatal depression find it hard to enjoy their new baby.

Unwanted pregnancy can be avoided when young people understand their relationships and are thoughtful about whether a relationship has reached a stage where starting to have sexual intercourse is right for them. Young couples need to be able to communicate their feelings and have confidence and trust in each other, and they also need practical knowledge in order to organize and use adequate contraception.

6 Avoiding pregnancy
Relationships and contraception

There are many ways of thinking about how to avoid unwanted pregnancy. We need to examine how we build relationships in which sex becomes important. We need to think about how we communicate within such a relationship to know when having sex will be right for us. Sadly, many teenagers regret the first time that they have sex, saying that they were not ready for it or even that they were too drunk to remember it. This really important part of your relationship does not have to be like this.

Relationships

When, as a teenager, you start to develop emotional and sexual relationships, your feelings have been influenced by all your past experiences of contact with other people – most likely starting with the very dependent relationship with your mother when you were first born. We are all brought up in a huge variety of ways and different cultures and religions. We may live with two birth parents, one parent, in a step family or in an extended family. Our attitudes to relationships are affected by those we have seen around us – which could mean parents developing an equal and caring relationship, happily kissing and cuddling in our company; or abusive relationships between the adults close to us; or unequal partnerships where one person physically or emotionally dominates the other.

Also, through childhood and adolescence, we develop skills of expressing our feelings within relationships. If we always bottle up our feelings, whether we are sad or happy, it becomes more and more difficult to share them with others. We need to learn to recognize the people with whom it is safe to share our feelings. To do that, we have to learn mutual trust. Some feelings and worries can be shared with our parents. Sometimes it is easier to confide in a trusted friend or a brother or sistcr. When, as teenagers, we start to develop more intimate relationships with just one person, we use all these 'interpersonal' skills that we have been learning.

Tony talks:
'It's difficult with
my mates. All the lads seem
to talk about at school is whether
you have had it off with someone yet. I'm
not sure they all have, even though they brag. But it
seems that sex is all that counts. I really like Tina.
She said she loved me once. It felt really
good. I really respect her. But I find it
really hard to know how to
tell her that I care for
her.'

Sexuality

So where does sex come into this? What happens at puberty that moves young people gradually from being happy playing children's games in the playground to wanting a one-to-one relationship with someone of the opposite sex? Young people are developing into adults, both emotionally and physically. As the external changes of puberty occur, the sex organs are also developing and producing the hormones that help to produce sex drive.

In boys this hormone is testosterone. During puberty many obvious things happen – hair grows under the arms, in the pubic area and on the face, the testicles and penis get bigger and the voice starts to break. But the presence of testosterone is also starting to stir other feelings. Boys start noticing that, when they think of something sexually attractive, they get an erection (the penis becomes bigger, stiff and upright). This can be embarrassing sometimes, for example when watching TV with friends and an erection develops at the sight of an attractive girl on the screen. Other things also start happening. During sexually exciting dreams boys can ejaculate (pump sperm and semen from the penis during an erection). Waking up after a so-called 'wet dream' with sticky, damp bed clothes can be alarming the first time it happens.

Obvious changes also happen to girls during puberty. Body shape changes, hips become broader, hair grows under the arms and in the pubic area, the breasts develop and periods start. In girls, the ovaries start producing the female hormones oestrogen and progesterone.

Sexual attraction means the desire to be very physically close to another person to whom you are attracted. When you are close, your feelings can be different from those you have experienced before. The feelings come from inside you. You start to feel excited, warm inside and tingly. Boys may develop an erection. Girls may notice the vagina becoming moist and warm. Dealing with these new

Crushes

First emotional attractions as teenagers can be very varied. It is very common to have 'crushes'. These are a safe way of testing out some of the strong emotions and feelings that are developing. You can have crushes on all sorts of people, from pop stars to senior students at school, from someone your own age and sometimes to your teachers. They can be on someone of the same sex or someone of the opposite sex.

New feelings

When we feel very close to someone, sexual feelings are aroused.

feelings can be both exciting and frightening. The feelings can be so strong that they drive young people on to have sexual intercourse without having thought about that possibility in advance. When intercourse occurs, pregnancy is always a possible outcome.

Safe sex

Strong feelings and desires lead young people into sexual relationships. How can you ensure that such a relationship does not lead to unwanted pregnancy or sexually transmitted infection?

There are many ways of having a physically satisfying and happy relationship without full penetrative sexual intercourse (i.e. ejaculation from the penis whilst fully entered into the vagina). Trying other things first helps you test the strength of your feelings for each other, and saves the extra-special loving bond of sex until you know that the relationship is right for you.

*Kissing, cuddling, stroking, massage and fondling are all sexy **and** safe. Exploring each other's bodies in these ways helps you to learn what feels safe and not threatening, and what feels good and exciting. It also helps you to know what feels aggressive and wrong.*

Many teenagers regret their first sexual activity. Many pressures make the idea of sex very attractive. You can feel pressurized by your friends. You may feel that if you have a girlfriend or boyfriend then you have to have sex. You may feel that your partner will leave you if you don't have sex. If you think that all your friends have already started sexual relationships, you may feel unhappy about being left behind. Magazines and films probably make sex look glamorous and exciting. Many teenagers sadly find that their first sexual experience occurred after drinking too much alcohol and they don't really remember it happening.

Understanding your feelings and being prepared to express your emotions can help you to be prepared and ready to develop a mature and satisfying relationship in which you have sex at the time that you are both ready for it. This will include having organized contraception to avoid unwanted pregnancy.

Double Dutch

This is a way of organizing contraception that is often advised particularly for young people. It involves using the pill or another form of contraception plus a condom. This has two advantages. First it makes contraception and therefore the avoidance of pregnancy even more reliable. Second it protects against sexually transmitted infections.

Contraception

Understanding sexual feelings and emotions prepares you to delay starting sexual relations until you are really ready. But when you do start having sex, how do you avoid pregnancy? Contraception (which literally means stopping conception) is the way couples try to prevent pregnancy despite having sexual intercourse. Different methods of contraception are:

Barrier contraception (putting a physical barrier between sperm and egg):
Male condoms are made of thin latex. They are rolled onto the erect penis just before insertion into the vagina. At ejaculation, the sperm and semen are trapped in the condom. Used properly, condoms are 94-98 per cent effective. They are the only form of contraception that also protects against sexually transmitted infection.

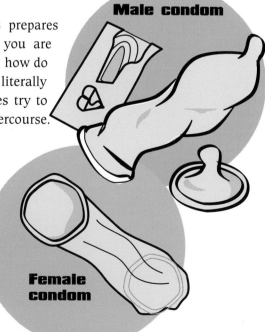

Male condom

Female condom

The **female condom** (or femidom) is made of thin polyurethane plastic. It is placed into the vagina and covers the area outside, stopping sperm entering the vagina. This contraceptive is 95 per cent effective.

The **diaphragm** or cap is dome-shaped and made of rubber. It is inserted into the vagina before sex, to cover the cervix. The correct size of cap has to be worked out after examination by a doctor or nurse. The cap is washed after use and can be re-used. It is 92-96 per cent effective.

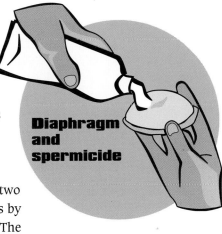

Diaphragm and spermicide

Hormonal methods of contraception (used by women):
The **combined pill** is made from a combination of the two female hormones, oestrogen and progesterone. It works by preventing the release of an egg from the ovary. The combined pill is prescribed by a doctor or nurse. It is not safe for everyone to use. Taking the pill can have other advantages such as reducing the effects of the premenstrual syndrome, reducing period pain, and making periods lighter and more regular. There are many types of this pill to suit different women's needs. It is 99 per cent effective.

Progesterone-only pill

The **progesterone-only pill** works by making the mucus of the cervix a more efficient barrier to sperm and by thinning the lining of the uterus to prevent implantation of a fertilized egg. It is useful for some women who are unable to take the combined pill for medical reasons and is 98 per cent effective. It must be prescribed by a doctor or nurse.

Combined pill

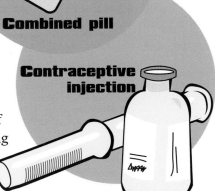

Contraceptive injection

A **contraceptive injection** is an injection of progesterone that releases a small amount of progesterone regularly into the body, thereby stopping ovulation. It has to be repeated every three months, but does avoid having to remember a daily pill. It is 99 per cent effective.

Intrauterine methods:
An **IUD** (intrauterine device) is a T-shaped plastic device with a coil of copper around the stem. It is inserted through the cervix and into the uterus by a doctor. It works by stopping sperm meeting the egg and/or by stopping the fertilized egg from implanting in the uterus. The IUD is not suitable for everyone. It is not usually advised for women who have never had a baby. It may make periods heavier and more painful. It is 98 per cent effective.

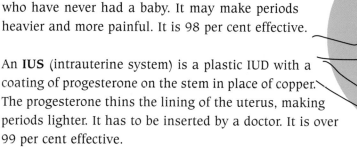

Intrauterine system

Intrauterine device

An **IUS** (intrauterine system) is a plastic IUD with a coating of progesterone on the stem in place of copper. The progesterone thins the lining of the uterus, making periods lighter. It has to be inserted by a doctor. It is over 99 per cent effective.

Natural methods
To practise this method of contraception, the woman must learn to recognize the stage of her menstrual cycle at which she ovulates. She then avoids intercourse at this stage of the cycle. For many women, particularly teenagers with irregular menstrual cycles, this is very difficult to predict. It is therefore not a very reliable form of contraception. There are devices that women who have a regular cycle can use to try to detect the timing of ovulation. The device detects hormone levels in the woman's urine. This method is only 94 per cent effective.

Emergency contraception
This is contraception that is used after unprotected sex. Unprotected sex is when no contraception has been used or when the method has failed (for example, a pill has been missed or the condom has burst). There

The emergency pill

The emergency contraceptive pill is often wrongly called the 'morning-after pill'. Emergency hormonal contraception can still be effective if used up to 72 hours after unprotected intercourse. However, the earlier it is used the more effective it is.

are two types of emergency hormonal contraception. The combined form is a high strength of the combined pill, taken in two doses 12 hours apart. It may work by stopping ovulation or by preventing implantation of the fertilized egg. It is 50 per cent effective if used after sex at the most fertile time of the menstrual cycle. The new form of emergency hormonal contraception is a progesterone-only form, again taken in two doses 12 hours apart. It works in a similar way but is more effective and has fewer side effects. It is nearly 75 per cent effective.

An emergency IUD can be inserted up to five days after unprotected intercourse and then used as a long-term method of contraception. It is 98 per cent effective.

Cultural and religious factors in contraception

It is not always morally possible for people to use all types of contraception. Different religions have guidance about the types of contraception that are acceptable. For example, the Catholic Church does not agree with any artificial forms of contraception. The only methods that should be used by practising Catholics are natural methods or abstinence. Termination of pregnancy is also not permissible. Islamic rule only allows the majority of forms of contraception to be used by married couples in order to space the children in a family. Other world religions, such as Hinduism, Judaism and Buddhism, also have rules about the types of contraception that are acceptable. If you are a devout practising member of a religion, then you will be aware of these teachings, or you can seek advice from your family or religious leaders.

The Catholic view

Catholic guidance about contraception and abortion is very strict. The head of the Catholic Church, the pope explains the Church's beliefs and teachings.

7 The Future
Increasing choices

Life will not stand still. Facilities for planning and managing your fertility will progress beyond what is available now.

Contraception

In the field of contraception, research constantly moves forward in trying to produce the optimum contraceptive that is safe, reliable and hazard-free. Advances are being made in barrier contraception to make a product that is effective and nicer to use than condoms and can be combined with chemical gels that may kill both sperm and viruses.

Hormonal contraception for women will continue to improve. New ways of giving it will be found, such as by patch: a sticky patch is attached to the skin and the hormone is absorbed through the skin. Maybe other chemicals will become available that need to be taken only once a month. The 'male pill' might be developed, finding a hormonal way to block sperm production.

The IUD is being refined, making it much smaller – effectively a single thread that can be attached to the inside of the uterus. This will make the IUD easier to use for women who have never had children.

IVF

A view through the microscope of a human egg being injected with sperm. On the left is a pipette used to hold the egg in place while the injection is carried out.

Maybe, in the future, methods will be found that can stop the production of either sperm or eggs until the man or woman wishes to be fertile. Other techniques, such as using chemicals that prevent the implantation of the fertilized egg in the uterus or possibly immunizing women against sperm, are in the early stages of investigation.

Fertility management

The pace of change in this area has been phenomenal. Fertility management is currently used to help couples who are having difficulty conceiving. Artificial means of solving the problem are becoming more and more successful. The most common is in vitro fertilization (IVF) – the development of a test-tube baby. The process involves extracting eggs from the woman's ovary, fertilizing them with the male sperm in the laboratory, and then implanting the fertilized egg into the woman's uterus.

The world's first successful test-tube baby was Louise Brown, born in Oldham, Lancashire, in 1978. Her birth gave hope to many infertile couples. Since then IVF has continued to advance. The success of the basic procedure opened the way to many possibilities for the future, moving the frontiers both scientifically and ethically.

Experimentation on the embryo before it is reimplanted in the uterus allows genetic manipulation. This will be used to help with the management of some inherited diseases but could also be used to allow couples to choose attributes in their offspring such as sex, eye colour etc. The science fiction·concept of the 'designer baby' may become a reality.

The baby who launched a revolution

LOUISE BROWN, the world's first test-tube child, is 21 ...

Doctor offers choice of baby's sex

A DOCTOR specializing in in vitro fertilization is to launch the world's first fertility service to create babies of whichever sex their parents require in return for fees of £8,000-£10,000.

Gay men expecting £2,000,000 twins

TWO wealthy gay men caused an angry response from family groups yesterday after bypassing British law to allow them to become the parents of surrogate twins, due to be born in the USA in December.

OLDER WOMEN AND IVF

A 63-year-old woman who lied about her age to get IVF treatment has become the oldest woman to give birth to a healthy baby. Her case has led to renewed questions of ethics and whether there should be an age limit on becoming a parent.

As women get older, their chance increases of having a baby affected by chromosomal abnormalities such as Down's syndrome. To avoid this, in the future, it may become possible for women to store ovarian tissue while they are young to use at a later date.

Further advances in fertility management, and perhaps also in the production of therapies for medical problems, may be possible by using the technique of cloning, which produced Dolly the sheep. The technique, otherwise known as 'cell nuclear transfer', involves taking an egg and removing its nucleus (the part of the cell containing genetic material). The nucleus is then replaced with the nucleus from an adult cell. Before the transfer the genetic material in the replacement nucleus could be manipulated to produce new characteristics in the offspring.

At the present time, cloning of humans has not occurred. Research is progressing fast in animals, with one of the motives being to produce animals that will be able to donate organs to humans for, for example, kidney

Dolly
Cloning produced Dolly the sheep in 1997.

transplantation. It may be possible to produce animals that will make blood products that can be used in humans.

A difficult ethical debate remains about the whole area, including the extension of cloning to humans. Many people have argued the case in favour of human cloning – for instance, to help infertile couples, to help lesbian women to have children, to produce a genetic replica of a child lost by stillbirth, illness or accident. Obviously, further debate will be needed to sort out how appropriate these ideas are for human life.

And the rest of the world

While the Western world is struggling with the issues that arise from what scientists are offering in the fields of biology and genetics, much of the rest of the world still lives in extreme poverty. World population growth is outstripping growth in food production.

A midwife
A UNICEF midwife visits a pregnant mother in a village in Malawi.

In 1994 an international conference held in Cairo investigated the problems of world population growth. From the origins of man until 1800 AD the world's human population grew to reach 1 billion. The next 5 billion people were added in 200 years. It has taken only 12 years for the last 1 billion people to be added. The size of the world's population has increased more in the last 50 years than in the previous million years!

The largest increase in population occurs in countries with the greatest poverty and unemployment. 97 per cent of future world population growth will be in developing countries, with the highest growth rate in Africa.

Governments around the world have responded in different ways to the problem of the rapidly increasing sizes of their populations. In the 1960s, the average family size in developing countries was 6 children. But advances in public health – particularly the availability of vaccinations against common infectious diseases – had made children much healthier, and far fewer family members were dying in childhood. It became important to find ways of slowing the growth of the population.

China developed its 'one child policy' in 1979. Families were given many incentives, including financial incentives and access to better housing and schools, to make them restrict their family to one child only. This policy was rapidly successful in reducing population growth: the number of births per woman fell on average from 6 children to 2 children over a period of only 20 years.

Other countries, such as Bangladesh and some in Africa, have achieved success in other ways. They have rapidly

Two approaches

China's 'one-child' policy was coercive. A softer approach, as in the Gambia, where health workers go out to explain contraception, may be just as successful in reducing the birth rate.

expanded access to contraception. They no longer need medical staff to administer contraception but sell it in shops, or use trained field workers to take contraception to people in rural villages. These techniques, in conjunction with improved education and expectations, particularly for young women, have really helped to reduce the birth rate.

On average, in the developing world, the number of births per woman has fallen during the last 30 years from 6 children to 3 children. But there are still huge variations around the world. Health risks are much higher in developing countries. In those countries 2 million children die every year of diseases that could be prevented by vaccination. 7.5 million children die per year as newborn babies because their mothers have received poor health care during pregnancy and childbirth. 200 million children are malnourished. 200 million poor people in the world have no access to contraception. Deaths of women related to pregnancy and childbirth are 250 times more common than in developed countries.

In the developed world we are fortunate. If we choose we can have access to contraception. We can choose our relationships and plan to have our children at stages in our lives that suit us. We can be much more confident that, when we have children, they will be healthy and live till old age. We have a duty to future generations to use all these advantages wisely.

Over to you

There are more teenagers in the world today than there have ever been before. Answers to questions about the future lie in your hands.

Resources

The following organizations provide information for young people about sexuality and pregnancy:

Brook Advisory Centres
165 Gray's Inn Road,
London WC1X 8UD

Young People's Information Line:
  0800 0185 023

- 🌀 24-hour recorded information can be heard by telephoning these numbers:

General	020 7617 8000
Emergency contraception	020 7617 0801
Missed a period?	020 7617 0802
Abortion	020 7617 0803
Starting contraception	020 7617 0804
Pregnant and unsure?	020 7617 0805
Visiting a Brook Centre	020 7617 0806
Sexually Transmitted Infections	020 7617 0807

- 🌀 Information leaflets include:
  Cool it! Guide to safe sex
  Cool Lover's Guide to Slick Condom Use
  Roll with it: a real guide to enjoying using condoms
  Helpful Hormones or Problem Pill: guide to hormonal contraception
  Wise Up – guide to sex advice services for young men
  Wise Up – guide to sex advice services for young women
  Answering Young People's Questions on Abortion

- 🌀 Website: The Site
  http://www.thesite.org.uk
  Young people's information on aspects of health, etc

Family Planning Association
2-12 Pentonville Road,
London N1 9FP

Telephone: 020 7837 4044

- 🌀 Information on all aspects of contraception, family planning services and sexual health.

- 🌀 Runs a network of local family planning clinics, whose contact numbers can be found in the phone directory under the heading 'Health Authority'.

- 🌀 Publishes leaflets:
  4 Girls: A Below-the-Bra Guide to the Female Body
  4 Boys: A Below-the-Belt Guide to the Male Body

Marie Stopes International
Marie Stopes House,
108 Whitfield Street,
London W1P 6BE

Telephone: 020 7388 0662

Information about contraception and termination of pregnancy.

British Pregnancy Advisory Service
Central telephone: 0845 730 4030

Information about pregnancy testing, abortion advice, emergency contraception.

GUM clinics
If you need information and advice about sexually transmitted infections, you can find the contact numbers of GUM clinics in the telephone directory or from your local hospital. The clinics may be listed as Sexually Transmitted Diseases Clinics, Special Clinics or Genitourinary Medicine (GUM) Clinics.

Recommended reading
Nicholas Allan, *The First Time*, Red Fox, 1995. (A book for boys to learn about sex)

Aidan Macfarlane and Ann McPherson, *The New diary of a teenage health freak*, Oxford Paperbacks, 1996

Sue Townsend, *The Secret Diary of Adrian Mole aged 13³/₄*, Arrow, 1982, 1998

Sex and the law in the UK

The legal age of consent for heterosexual relationships is 16 years.

If a woman under 16 years has sex, it is the male partner who is committing an offence.

The minimum age for marriage is 16 years (those under 18 require parental consent in England and Wales).

There is no age limit for legal abortion.

Girls under 16 can be prescribed contraception if the doctor is satisfied that they are mature enough to understand the consequences.

Young people under 16 as well as at any other age are entitled to confidential care – i.e. their parents do not have to be informed.

Glossary

antenatal care	medical and nursing care given to women during pregnancy, to look after them and the developing baby.
conception	the joining of sperm and egg to start a pregnancy.
congenital abnormality	an abnormality caused by damage to the developing fetus in the uterus.
contraception	methods used to avoid conception or, in other words, to avoid pregnancy despite having sexual intercourse.
embryo	the very early cellular stage of development of a baby in the uterus.
fertility	a person's ability to conceive.
fetus	the fully developed baby still growing in the uterus.
hormone	chemical messenger produced in a gland in the body.
labour	the process of contraction of the uterus to push the baby down through the vagina, to give birth.
midwife	nurse who looks after women during pregnancy and delivery and immediately after birth.
obstetrician	doctor who specializes in looking after pregnancy and delivery.
ovary	female gonad or site of production of eggs and the female hormones oestrogen and progesterone.
ovulation	the release of an egg from the ovary.
ovum	the female gamete or seed.
postnatal care	medical and nursing care given to mothers and babies after delivery.
postnatal depression	depression that occurs in the months after giving birth to a baby.
pregnancy test	method of detecting pregnancy hormones present in a woman's urine, in order to confirm pregnancy.
safe sex	having sex and sexual satisfaction but taking precautions to avoid getting pregnant and catching sexually transmitted infections.
sexually transmitted infection	infection that can only be caught by sexual contact.
sperm	the male gamete or seed.
spontaneous abortion	medical term for miscarriage, when the pregnancy is lost naturally.
testis	male gonad or site of production of sperm and the male hormone testosterone.
therapeutic abortion	medically known as a termination of pregnancy: the ending of a pregnancy so that it does not result in the birth of a baby.
ultrasound scan	test using sound waves to take a picture of the baby in the uterus.

Index

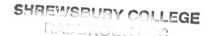
Note on case studies
Photographs illustrating the case studies in this book were posed by models.